Oceans and Seas

Mediterranean Sea

John F. Prevost

ABDO Publishing Company

visit us at
www.abdopub.com

Published by ABDO Publishing Company, 4940 Viking Drive, Edina, Minnesota 55435.

Printed in the United States.

Contributing Editors: Kate A. Conley, Kristin Van Cleaf, Kristianne E. Vieregger
Photo Credits: Corbis
Art Direction & Maps: Neil Klinepier

Library of Congress Cataloging-in-Publication Data

Prevost, John F.
Mediterranean Sea / by John F. Prevost.
p. cm. -- (Oceans and seas)
Includes index.
Summary: Surveys the origin, geological borders, climate, water, plant and animal life, and economic and ecological aspects of the Mediterranean Sea.
ISBN 1-57765-097-2
1. Mediterranean Sea--Juvenile literature. [1. Mediterranean Sea.] I. Title. II. Series: Prevost, John F. Oceans and seas.
GC651.P74 1999
551.46'2--dc21 98-29320
CIP
AC

Contents

Mediterranean Sea

Six million years ago, Earth contained a desert that was as hot as Death Valley and three times deeper than the Grand Canyon. Today, that desert is the Mediterranean **Sea**!

The Atlantic Ocean's water flooded the Mediterranean's dry basin about 5.5 million years ago. At that time, what is now the Strait of Gibraltar was a section of land. It separated the Mediterranean from the Atlantic Ocean. This land broke apart, causing Earth's largest waterfall. Water from the Atlantic flooded the desert, turning it into a huge sea.

Today, the Mediterranean is the world's largest inland sea. It separates Africa and Europe. It stretches from the Atlantic Ocean to Asia. Several countries border it. Many other seas are a part of the Mediterranean Sea.

THE MEDITERRANEAN SEA

Land Below the Sea

The Mediterranean **Sea** covers 970,000 square miles (2.5 million sq km). The Strait of Gibraltar connects the Atlantic Ocean and the Mediterranean Sea. The strait is narrow and shallow. Its narrowest point is only eight miles (13 km) wide.

The Mediterranean's basin is almost entirely landlocked. Its floor contains underwater mountain ranges and volcanoes. Some rise above the surface, creating many small islands. Some of these islands are Sicily, Crete, and Cyprus.

One large mountain range stretches between Sicily and northern Africa. This range divides the Mediterranean's basin. The Mediterranean's deepest point is east of the range. This point is 16,160 feet (4,926 m) below **sea level**.

Volcanic eruptions and earthquakes are frequent in the Mediterranean. These events have been occurring in this area for thousands of years. They continue to change the shape of the land.

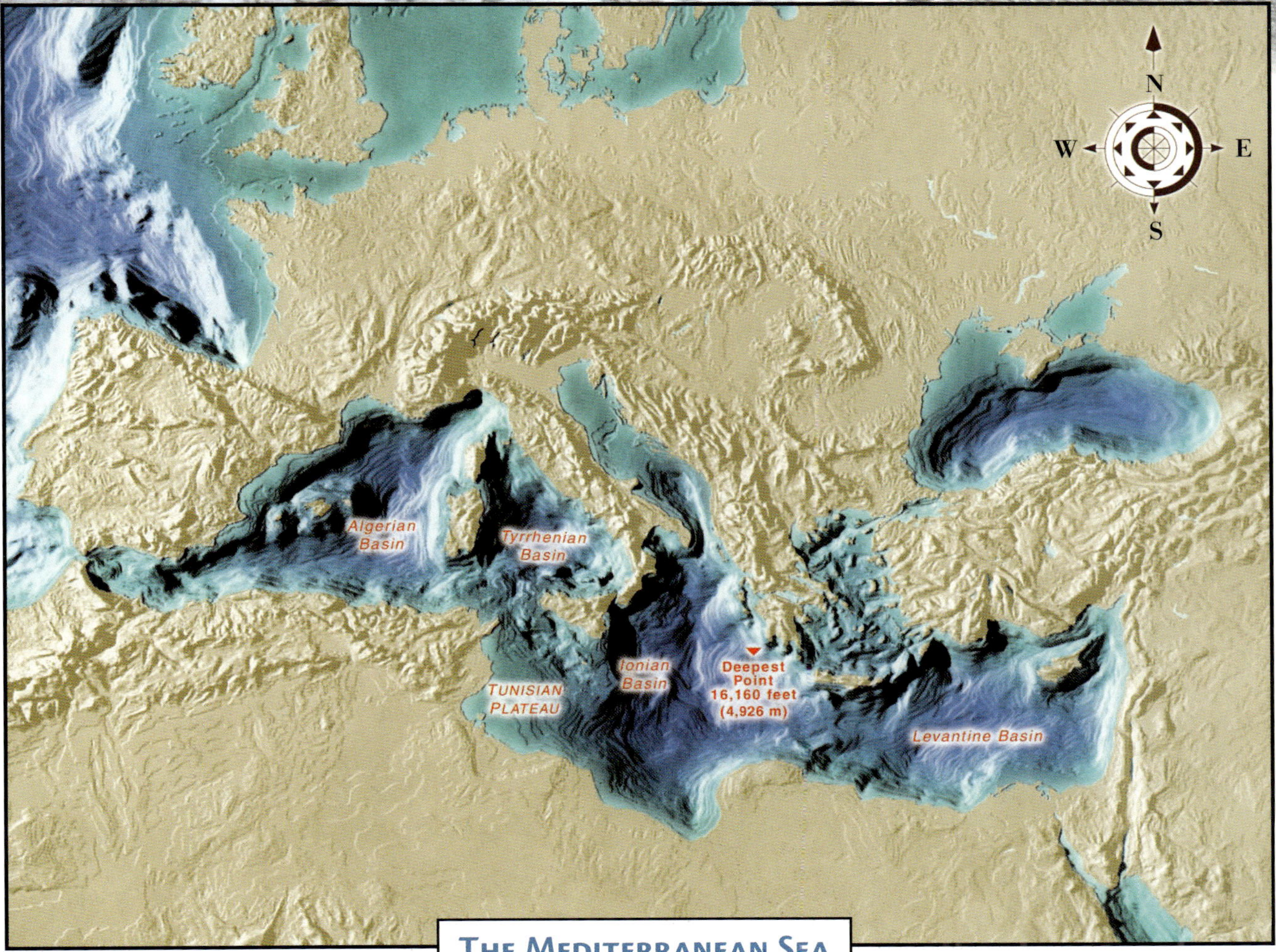

THE MEDITERRANEAN SEA

The Climate

The Mediterranean Sea's coastline is 29,000 miles (46,000 km) long.

The Mediterranean **Sea** and its coasts have mild weather all year. In the winter, many storms occur in the north and west. They are rarely serious and don't cause much damage. They provide most of the rain for the entire year.

In the summer, certain areas of the Mediterranean Sea may have several months without any rain. The south and east areas of the sea are nearest to the **equator**. Therefore, they have hotter, drier summers than other areas of the Mediterranean.

The Mediterranean's water reaches its highest surface temperatures in August. At that time, temperatures can reach

88°F (31°C). The coldest temperatures occur in February, when surface temperatures can drop to 41°F (5°C). Ice can form in some areas of the **sea**. But temperatures rarely drop below freezing.

The Strait of Gibraltar, with Spain's coast in the foreground and Africa's coast in the background

The Water

Most of the Mediterranean **Sea**'s water comes from the Atlantic Ocean. It enters the Mediterranean through the Strait of Gibraltar.

The Mediterranean's water level is about 6 inches (15 cm) lower than that of the Strait of Gibraltar. For this reason, a steady current flows into the Mediterranean from the Atlantic. This current flows east along the northern coast of Africa. It also flows north across the sea.

Some of the Mediterranean Sea's water sinks to form the Mediterranean Intermediate Water. Eventually, this water flows back into the Atlantic Ocean. Water also enters the Mediterranean from the Black Sea. The Suez Canal connects the Mediterranean to the Red Sea.

The Mediterranean's water moves between the sea and the continents in the hydrologic cycle. The Mediterranean's hot, dry climate causes the sea's water to evaporate quickly. The evaporated water later cools and falls to Earth as rain. The rain collects in rivers, such as the Nile, Ebro, Po, and Rhône. These rivers drain into the Mediterranean **Sea**.

THE HYDROLOGIC CYCLE

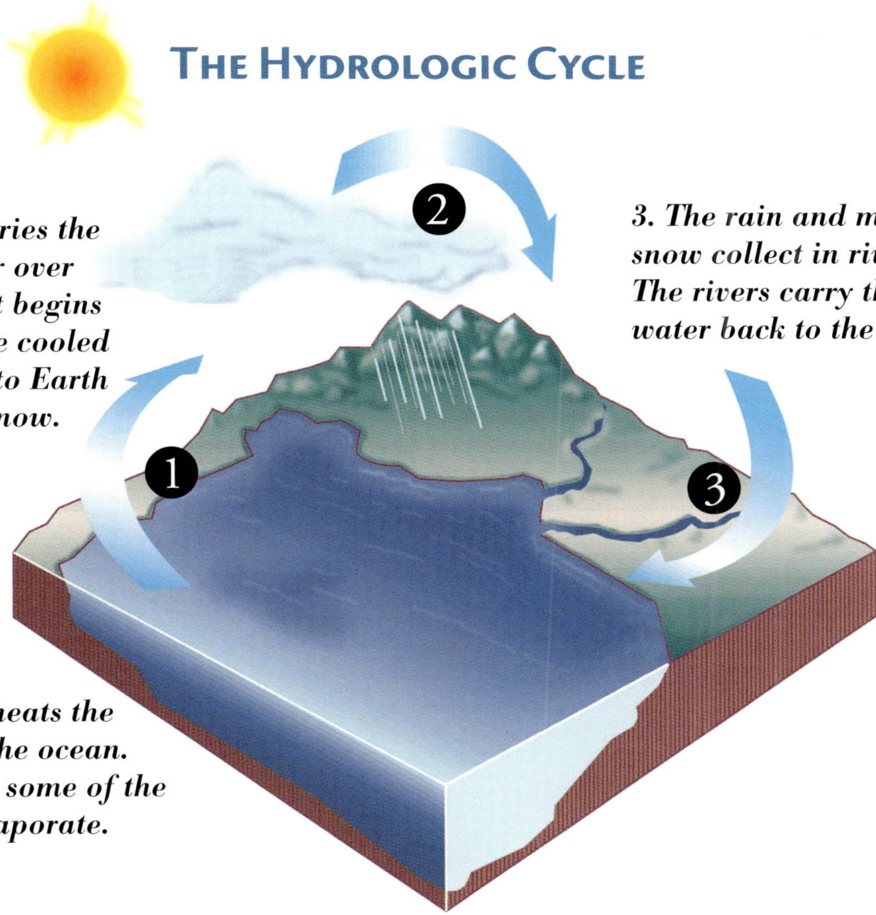

2. Wind carries the water vapor over land until it begins to cool. The cooled water falls to Earth as rain or snow.

3. The rain and melted snow collect in rivers. The rivers carry the water back to the ocean.

1. The sun heats the surface of the ocean. This causes some of the water to evaporate.

Plants

The Mediterranean **Sea**'s water contains large amounts of salt, but few nutrients. This makes it difficult for plants to survive in the water. Despite this, a large variety of plants have adapted to the Mediterranean Sea's conditions.

Most plants in the Mediterranean Sea live near the surface of the water. They do this because they need sunlight for **photosynthesis**. Plants that float in the sea are called phytoplankton. They form the base of the **food chain**.

Another group of plants that live in the sea are algae, sometimes called seaweeds. These larger plants provide shelter and food for many sea animals. Most algae are attached to the sea's floor.

The Mediterranean's hot, dry climate prevents many plants from growing along the shore. However, some plants, such as olive trees, have adapted to the weather.

This diver is studying seaweed in the Mediterranean Sea.

Animals

A variety of animals live in the Mediterranean **Sea**. But the number of fish, marine mammals, and reptiles has been greatly reduced by **overfishing** and pollution. And some of the remaining animals are **endangered**.

Mediterranean reptiles include green and loggerhead sea turtles. They are endangered, but because of new protection laws, these species may be able to survive.

There are about 400 species of fish in the Mediterranean. Some of these include flounder, lizardfish, gobies, and even sharks. Sponges and corals are also plentiful.

Mediterranean monk seals have been living in the Mediterranean longer than humans. Fishers used to kill the seals because they thought these animals ate too many fish. Today, there are fewer than 400 Mediterranean monk seals left.

Crabs, such as this one, live deep in the sea.

A diver stands behind a dolphin in the Mediterranean Sea.

People & Cultures

The Mediterranean **Sea** is often called the cradle of western civilization. People have lived along its shores for thousands of years. Today, many different countries border the sea. Each country has its own distinctive **culture** and history.

The Egyptians were probably the first people to settle around the Mediterranean Sea. They had a national government as early as 3100 B.C. By the A.D. 100s, the Roman Empire ruled all of the lands that bordered the sea. They called the sea *Mare Nostrum,* which means Our Sea.

The arena inside the Colosseum

These **cultures**, as well as several others, left behind landmarks such as the Pyramids in Egypt and the Colosseum in Italy. They also left their languages, religions, and laws to the people living there today.

The Colosseum was built almost 2,000 years ago.

Economy

The Mediterranean **Sea** has many valuable natural resources. Many Mediterranean people earn their living by catching fish. Popular catches include anchovies, sardines, and bluefin tuna.

This sea also provides transportation routes for people and materials. The Suez Canal opened in 1869. It connects the Mediterranean with the Red Sea and the Indian Ocean. This greatly reduced the shipping time between Europe and the Middle East.

People have taken salt from the sea's waters for many years. Recently, interest has grown in undersea exploration and mining. People now collect oil, natural gas, and mineral deposits from beneath the seafloor.

Tourism is a major source of income for many countries bordering the sea. More than half of the world's tourism income is from the Mediterranean Sea. Millions of people visit this region every year to enjoy its rich **culture** and beautiful weather.

Tourists snorkel over a coral reef in the Mediterranean Sea.

Mediterranean Future

Overfishing has caused the near extinction of several species of fish, **sea** turtles, and seals in the Mediterranean Sea. In addition, fishers still use a type of net that catches too many young, small fish. This prevents the fish population from growing. So the Mediterranean region now has to import fish for food.

Pollution is another problem for the Mediterranean Sea. Pollution along the coast, such as **sewage** and litter, kills many animals every year. The large number of people that visit and live near the Mediterranean add to the area's pollution.

In 1975, 16 countries bordering the Mediterranean Sea approved the Mediterranean Action Plan. People still follow this plan today. Its goal is to improve the environmental conditions of the Mediterranean Sea. With the help of this plan, people will be able to enjoy the Mediterranean Sea for years to come.

People are working to preserve the Mediterranean Sea's coastline by cleaning sites such as this waste dump.

Glossary

culture - the customs, arts, and tools of a nation or people at a certain time.

endangered - to put in danger of becoming extinct.

equator - an imaginary circle around the middle of Earth.

food chain - an arrangement of plants and animals in a community. Each plant or animal feeds on other plants and animals in a certain order. For example, phytoplankton are eaten by small fish, small fish are eaten by larger fish, and large fish are eaten by humans.

overfish - to catch so many fish that the number of fish in a given body of water is greatly reduced.

photosynthesis - the process by which green plants use light energy, carbon dioxide, and water to make food and oxygen.

sea - a body of water that is smaller than an ocean and is almost completely surrounded by land.

sea level - the average height of all the oceans. It is often used to measure height or depth, with sea level as zero feet.

sewage - waste matter carried off by sewers.

How Do You Say That?

algae - AL-gee
Colosseum - kah-luh-SEE-uhm
Cyprus - SI-pruhs
Gibraltar - juh-BRAWL-tuhr
hydrologic - hi-dro-LAH-jihk
Mediterranean - meh-duh-tuh-RAY-nee-uhn
photosynthesis - foh-toh-SIN-thuh-suhs
phytoplankton - fi-toh-PLANGK-tuhn
Sicily - SIH-suh-lee

Web Sites

Would you like to learn more about the Mediterranean Sea? Please visit **www.abdopub.com** to find up-to-date Web site links about the Mediterranean's history, people, and wildlife. These links are routinely monitored and updated to provide the most current information available.

Index